Origami for Diwali

ORIGAMI HOLIDAYS

Robyn Hardyman

PowerKiDS press.

New York

Published in 2017 by **The Rosen Publishing Group, Inc.**
29 East 21st Street, New York, NY 10010

Cataloging-in-Publication Data

Names: Hardyman, Robyn.
Title: Origami for Diwali / Robyn Hardyman.
Description: New York : PowerKids Press, 2017. | Series: Origami holidays | Includes index.
Identifiers: ISBN 9781508151104 (pbk.) | ISBN 9781508151043 (library bound) | ISBN 9781508150923 (6 pack)
Subjects: LCSH: Origami--Juvenile literature. | Divali--Juvenile literature.
Classification: LCC TT870.H37 2017 | DDC 736'.982--dc23

Produced for Rosen by Calcium Creative Ltd
Editors for Calcium Creative Ltd: Sarah Eason and Jennifer Sanderson
Designers: Paul Myerscough and Jessica Moon
All origami photography by Jessica Moon

Picture credits: Cover: Shutterstock: Tania Anisimova, Natis76. Insides: Shutterstock: Tania Anisimova throughout, Anshu18 25, Christos Georghiou 13, JOAT 6–7, Marina Kuchugurova throughout, Rich Lindie 7, Natis76 throughout, Alexander Ryabintsev throughout, Raksha Shelare 12–13, Nataliia Sokolovska 18–19, SMDSS 19, Starcreative throughout, Szefei 4–5, Zzvet 24–25.

Manufactured in the United States of America

CPSIA Compliance Information: Batch #BS16PK: For Further Information contact Rosen Publishing, New York, New York at 1-800-237-9932

Contents

Diwali 4

Festival of Light 6

    Diya Lamp 8

    Diwali Lantern 10

A New Year 12

    Candy Box 14

    Pretty Wallet 16

Diwali Decorations 18

    Garland Flower 20

    Flower Vase 22

Celebrating Diwali 24

    Diwali Dog 26

    Colorful Candle 28

Glossary 30

Further Reading 31

Index 32

Diwali

Diwali is a festival of light that is celebrated as part of the **Hindu** faith. It is celebrated in October or November and it lasts for up to five days. There are more than one billion Hindus around the world. Hindus believe there is one god, Brahman, but that he takes many different forms. These forms include King Rama, the **goddess** Lakshmi, and the goddess Kali. At Diwali, Hindus remember the story of Rama and his wife Sita. They also honor Lakshmi and Kali. Many Hindus celebrate Diwali as the start of a new year, too.

Diwali is a festival of light, and people use these traditional clay lamps filled with oil to decorate homes and **temples**.

Folds and Bases

These instructions explain how to make the main folds and bases you will use for your origami activities.

Valley fold: To make a valley fold, fold the paper toward you.

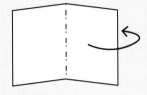

- - - - - - - -

Mountain fold: To make a mountain fold, fold the paper away from you.

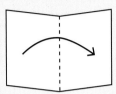

- ⋅ - ⋅ - ⋅ -

Turn over the model

Rotate the model

Cut with scissors

Push or pull in this direction

Square Base

Blintz Base

Waterbomb Base

A Great King

Long ago, a prince named Rama was married to Sita. He was prince of the kingdom of Ayodhya, but he and Sita were **exiled** by his wicked **stepmother**. Sita was then kidnapped by Ravana, an evil king. Rama fought a great battle with Ravana. Finally, after 14 years, Rama returned to Ayodhya with Sita, and was crowned king. It was a dark night, so people lit their way with lamps. At Diwali, Hindus celebrate Rama's triumphant return, as a victory of good over evil.

In this book you will find out how to make some wonderful origami pieces that will make Diwali even more fun and festive!

Happy Diwali!

Kite Base

Squash Fold

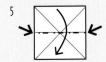

Festival of Light

Diwali means "row of lights." It may also be spelled "Divali" or "Deepavali." A "diya" is a small clay lamp filled with oil. To celebrate Diwali, people put rows of lamps and lights in the doorways and windows of their homes. The lights are to remember the return of Rama and Sita to Ayodhya. They are also to welcome Lakshmi, the goddess of wealth, into their homes. Outside, the streets are lit with fairy lights, especially the stores and temples. Everything is ready for the festival to begin. Once Diwali has begun, people continue to fill their lives with light. They light sparklers and hold firework displays, and they keep the lamps burning throughout the festival.

This **murti** is of Ganesh, the elephant-headed deity.

Ganesh is a god of wisdom, success, and good luck.

Bringing Good Luck

In India, Hindus place diya lamps and flowers on large leaves and set them afloat on the Ganges River. They hope that if the lamps float all the way across this wide river, it will bring them good luck in the year ahead.

Prayers and Gifts

Diwali is a religious festival, and prayer is an important part of it. Hindus pray at home in the morning and evening, in front of murtis of their **deities**. They also visit the temple. There, the murtis are decorated with flowers, brightly colored clothes, and jewelry. People leave gifts of fruit, flowers, and candies for the murtis, and say prayers.

Diya Lamp

Make this little diya lamp, then make some more in different bright colors to decorate the dining table for Diwali. Put your lamps in a wide, shallow bowl to make a beautiful **centerpiece**.

1 Put your paper colored side up and make a kite base. Turn over your model.

2 Valley fold down the top of your model, and unfold.

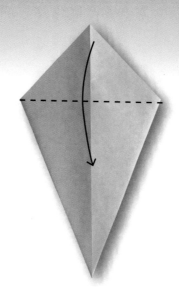

3 Valley fold the top down again to the crease made in step 2.

4 Valley fold the top down again to the crease made in step 2.

5 Valley fold the top down along the crease made in step 2.

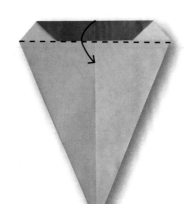

6 Mountain fold the bottom of your model. Make sure the triangle point is visible at the top of your model once the fold is completed.

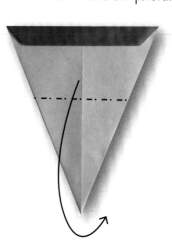

7 Give your model shape by mountain folding the left and right sides.

8 Your model should now look like this. Turn over your model.

9 Valley fold the bottom left and right sides into the center.

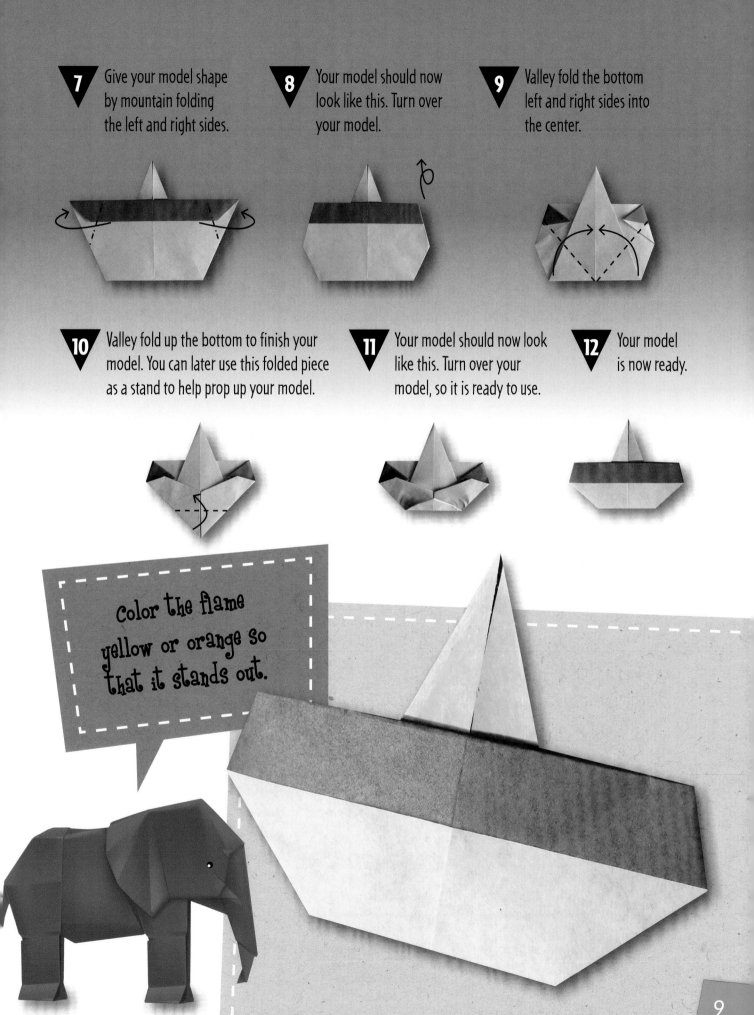

10 Valley fold up the bottom to finish your model. You can later use this folded piece as a stand to help prop up your model.

11 Your model should now look like this. Turn over your model, so it is ready to use.

12 Your model is now ready.

Color the flame yellow or orange so that it stands out.

Diwali Lantern

This lantern makes a perfect decoration for Diwali. It is simple to make so you can make a few in different colors for a great effect.

1 Start with a blintz base. Turn over your model and rotate your model 45 degrees.

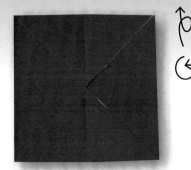

2 Valley fold the top and bottom points into the center.

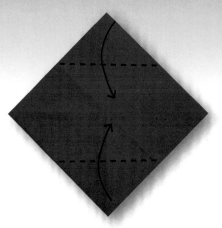

3 Your model should now look like this. Turn over your model.

4 Valley fold the left and right sides into the center.

5 Valley fold all four corners into the center.

6 Your model should now look like this. Turn over your model.

7 Your model should now look like this. Valley fold the two center triangles, opening them up as you do, and flattening out the sides to make a rectangle. This is a squash fold.

Close-up of squash fold

8 Your model is now complete. This is the front of your model.

Make a hole at the top of the lantern and thread through some string to hang it up!

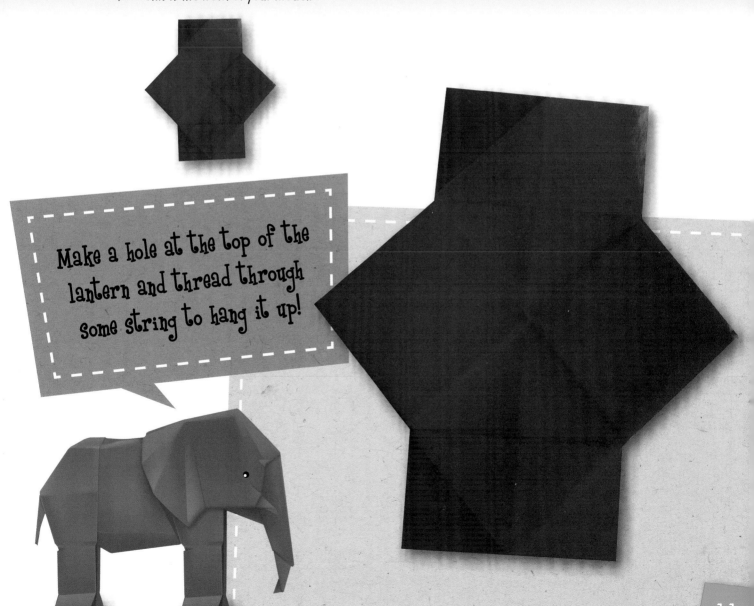

A New Year

The Hindu goddess Lakshmi symbolizes wealth. She is worshiped at Diwali. People believe she roams the world at this time, and will enter houses that are clean, pure, and brightly lit. People hope she will bless them with good luck and wealth.

The Great Goddess Lakshmi

In India, murtis of Lakshmi are carried through the streets in a fun and colorful **procession**. People want to thank Lakshmi for helping them earn money. They give gifts of candies and coins to each other, and leave **offerings** for Lakshmi in the temple.

Lamps and offerings of flowers and food are left for the goddess Lakshmi.

Wealth and Success

At Diwali, business people try to pay all their bills before the new **financial** year begins. They hope Lakshmi will favor them with success in business in the year ahead. Families also give children money at Diwali.

Thank you, Lakshmi!

Celebrating Everywhere

Diwali is a time for the whole community to celebrate, and all over the world Hindus gather to enjoy Diwali. There are wonderful public firework displays, and everyone sets off firecrackers and lights sparklers, too. It is a very noisy occasion! People put on plays about the story of Rama and Sita, and there is music and dancing in the streets. In traditional dances, the costumes are bright and colorful, and the dancers are very beautiful.

People leave offerings to Lakshmi so she will give them her blessings in the year to come.

Candy Box

This little star box is perfect for holding candies.

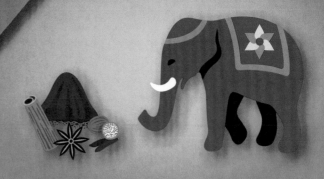

1 Start with a square base with the open points at the top. Valley fold the left and right sides into the center, and unfold.

Open points at top

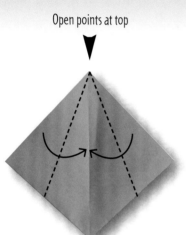

2 Valley fold the left and right points to the crease just made, and then unfold.

3 Lift and open the top left and right flaps. Press down to flatten the flaps.

Close-up of squash fold

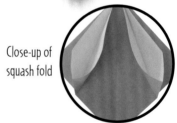

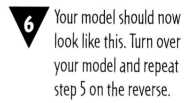

4 Your model should now look like this. Turn over your model and repeat steps 1, 2, and 3 on the reverse.

5 Your model should now look like this. Mountain fold the top left and right sides back behind themselves.

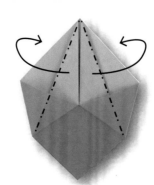

6 Your model should now look like this. Turn over your model and repeat step 5 on the reverse.

14

7 Your model should now look like this. Valley fold the bottom up and then unfold.

8 Valley fold down the top flap.

9 Valley fold the top left flap over to the right.

10 Your model should now look like this. Valley fold the top flap down as you did in step 8.

11 Turn over your model. Repeat step 8, and then steps 9 and 10 on this side.

12 Your model should now look like this on both sides. Open up the top of your model, smooth the sides, and flatten the base to create your box.

Open model here

You can use this box to store nuts, too.

Pretty Wallet

Make this cute little wallet to hold the coins that are given at Diwali.

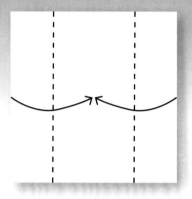

1 Start with your paper colored side down. Valley fold the left side over to the right, and unfold.

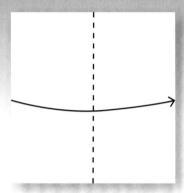

2 Valley fold the left and right sides into the center, and then unfold.

3 Valley fold the top of your paper down to the bottom.

4 Valley fold the top left and right corners, and then unfold.

5 Valley fold the upper left and right flaps into the center. Squash the top left and right points as you make the folds.

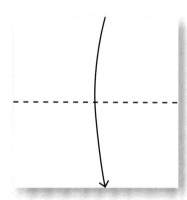

Close-up of squash fold

6 Your model should now look like this. Mountain fold the left and right sides.

7 Valley fold the upper bottom left and right flaps into the center.

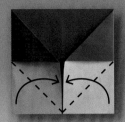

8 Valley fold the bottom triangle point up.

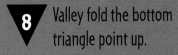

9 Valley fold this flap up again.

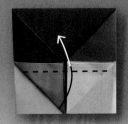
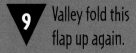

10 Your model should now look like this. Turn over your model and repeat step 7 with the bottom left and right flaps. Repeat steps 8 and 9 on this side.

11 Your model is now complete. Rotate it 180 degrees to start using it as your wallet.

You could also put coins in this pretty wallet and give it to a loved one.

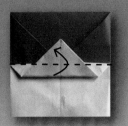
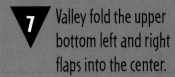

17

Diwali Decorations

At Diwali, everyone wants their home to look its best to welcome the deities. Homes are cleaned and decorated so they look beautiful. People hang up colored banners, paper chains, and strings of flowers. Lit diyas and flowers are placed in bowls of water, and put around the home. People also send greeting cards to wish others "Happy Diwali." Workplaces can be decorated, too. Dozens of pretty diya lamps may be put outside office buildings.

Colorful lanterns and flowers bring good luck and peace during Diwali.

Dressing Up

It is also important for people to look their best at Diwali. It is a time when many people buy new clothes to wear at the celebrations. Families give each other presents of new clothes, and it is a good time to buy new jewelry. Women and girls also decorate their hands and feet with special patterns called **mehndi**. They are painted on with a dye called **henna**.

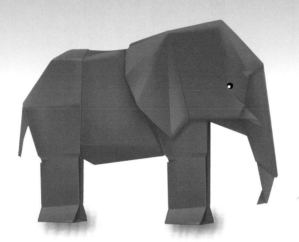

Beautiful Diwali!

Pretty Patterns and Designs

The entrances to homes and temples are decorated with special patterns called **rangoli**. These are to bring good luck and welcome the goddess Lakshmi. To make them, people dip their fingers in flour or ground rice, and colored powders, and paint the ground. Flower designs are very popular, but others such as fish, birds, and shapes such as circles and squares are used, too.

Garland Flower

You could make lots of these flowers to decorate a **mantel**.

1 Start with a waterbomb base. Fold your model in half, from left to right.

2 Valley fold the top right layer and then unfold.

3 Lift the top right layer, opening gently, and pressing to squash flat.

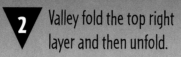

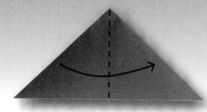

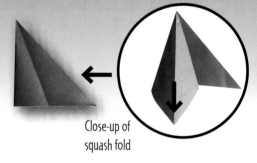

Close-up of squash fold

4 Your model should now look like this. Valley fold the top section over to the left. Then repeat steps 2 and 3 on the three remaining layers.

5 Valley fold the two top right flaps over to the left. Turn your model over and valley fold the top right flap over to the left. There should now be equal flaps on each side.

6 Your model should look like this. Valley fold the left and right sides into the center, and then unfold.

7 Lift the upper bottom layer to the top point of your model. Press the sides as you fold so they lie flat.

8 Your model should look like this. Turn over your model and repeat steps 6 and 7 on the reverse.

9 Your model should now look like this. Valley fold the left side over to the right and then repeat steps 6 and 7.

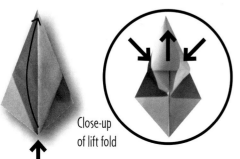

Close-up of lift fold

10 Your model should look like this. Valley fold the far right top flap over to the left. Repeat steps 6 and 7 on this final side.

11 Your model should now look like this. Valley fold down the top point. Repeat on all four sides, valley folding the flaps to the left. You should have equal flaps once all four sides are folded.

12 Rotate your model 180 degrees so that the open points are at the top.

13 Valley fold the upper left and right flaps into the center.

14 Repeat step 13 on the three remaining sides of your model.

15 Valley fold each of the top points down to create your petals.

Add a stem by attaching a straw to the bottom of your flower with tape or glue.

Flower Vase

Make the flowers from the previous page and put them in this vase.

1 Start with a large piece of paper. Valley fold and mountain fold your paper to divide it into three equal parts, and then unfold.

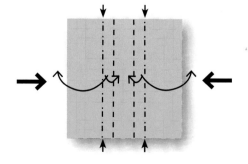

2 Valley fold your model three times as shown, and unfold.

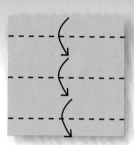

3 Valley fold your model four times as shown, and unfold.

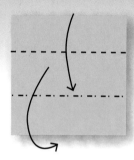

4 Rotate your model 90 degrees. Repeat steps 1 to 3. Your model should now look like this.

5 Valley fold and mountain fold both sides, then bring them into the center so the two mountain folds meet.

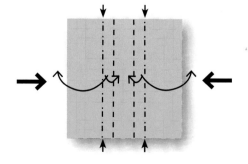

6 Valley fold and mountain fold the top and bottom, then bring them into the center so the two mountain folds meet.

7 Your model should look like this. Turn over your model.

8 Your model should now look like this. Lift the outer edges of the cross section and valley fold in. Squash the paper as you fold.

9 Your model should now look like this. Mountain fold the left and right sides back.

10 Mountain fold the top and bottom, turning over your model as you do, and tucking the ends behind the pockets.

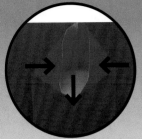

Close-up of squash fold

Close-up of tuck fold

11 Your model should now look like this. Turn over your model.

12 Now gently pull the four upper sections out to complete the vase.

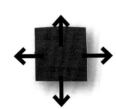

13 Your model should look like this. Turn over your model. It is now ready to use.

This vase will make a lovely centerpiece for your Diwali celebrations.

Celebrating Diwali

Around the world, Hindus have different **traditions** for celebrating the festival of Diwali. For example, in Nepal in South-Central Asia, Diwali is called Tihar or Swanti. Dogs and cows are dressed with flowers and ribbons, and given special treats. Dogs have a special bond with people, and cows are seen as symbols of **prosperity** and wealth. Crows and ravens are also given offerings, to prevent grief and death from entering the home.

These Nepalese girls are celebrating Diwali. They are dressed in their best costumes. The streets of their town, Pokhara, are decorated with lights and flowers, too.

Different Faiths

Members of the Sikh and Jain faiths also celebrate Diwali. For both groups, Diwali festivals last for three days. People dress in new clothes and give each other candies, as Hindus do. Sikhs celebrate the time when their sixth holy teacher, or **Guru**, named Har Gobind, was freed from prison. In the holy city of Amritsar, he was welcomed home with lamps and candles. Sikhs go to pray at their places of worship, called **gurdwaras**, which are lit with candles. In their homes, there is a lot of music and dancing.

Festive Food

Food is an important part of the Diwali celebrations. Hindus come together to feast with family and friends. They enjoy special fried savory dishes, such as **samosas**, and sweet desserts made with milk, sugar, and dried fruits. Children may also be given special candies made in the shape of diyas.

Celebrate together!

Remembering Lord Mahavira

Jains remember their spiritual leader, Lord Mahavira. They decorate their homes and temples with lights, and share candies with each other. They avoid firecrackers because they may harm living things. Jains believe it is important not to harm any living creature.

Jains gather in their temples to pray and to recite parts of their religious texts.

Diwali Dog

During Diwali in Nepal, to celebrate the special relationship between dogs and people, dogs are decorated and worshiped for one day.

1 Start with a kite base with the small triangle at the bottom. Turn over your paper.

2 Valley fold your paper in half.

3 Valley fold the upper triangle flap to the top.

4 Your model should look like this. Turn over your model.

5 Valley fold the top and bottom sections.

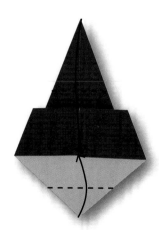

6 Valley fold the top and bottom triangle flaps.

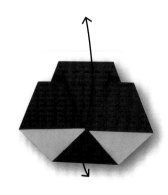

7 Valley fold down the top triangle.

8 Valley fold the right side over to the left.

9 Rotate your model 45 degrees counterclockwise.

10 Your model should now look like this. Valley fold the upper left flap over to the right, at the same time folding back the rear left flap.

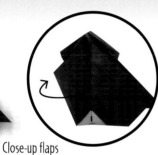

Close-up flaps folding back

11 Adjust the tail and the snout of your dog by pulling gently. Open the legs slightly to stand the model upright.

12 Your dog is now ready.

Use a marker to add features to the dog.

Colorful Candle

This candle uses a kind of origami that includes cutting. This is called **kirigami**. Make this candle to remind you that Diwali is a festival of light!

1 Start with your paper colored side up. Valley fold your paper in half, and then unfold.

2 Valley fold the left and right sides to the center.

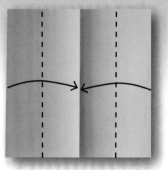

3 Valley fold the left and right sides into the center again, crease well.

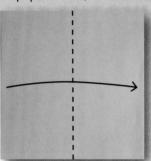

4 Unfold all the folds made in steps 2 and 3.

5 Your paper should now look like this. Valley fold down the top of your paper, and then unfold.

6 Make four cuts using a pair of scissors.

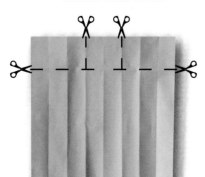

7 Your model should now look like this. Repeat steps 2 and 3 on the lower part of your paper.

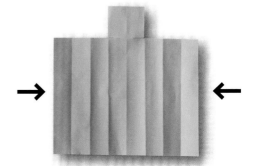

8 Valley fold the left and right sides of the lower part. Mountain fold the left and right sides of the upper part of your model.

9 Your model should now look like this. Turn over your model.

10 Valley fold the edges of the top section to create your flame.

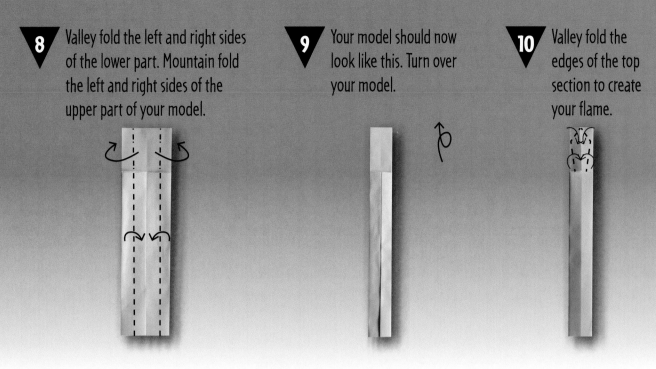

11 Your model should now look like this. Turn over your model.

12 Your model is now ready.

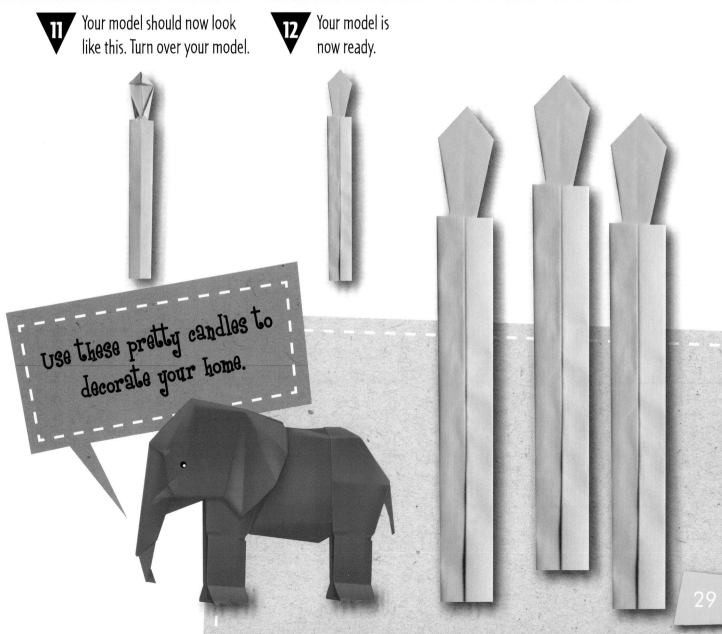

Use these pretty candles to decorate your home.

Glossary

centerpiece A decoration for the middle of a table.

deities Gods or goddesses.

exiled Forced to leave a country to live in a foreign country.

financial To do with money.

goddess Female spirit or being that has great power, strength, and knowledge.

gurdwaras Sikh temples.

Guru A Sikh holy teacher.

henna A red-brown dye made from the henna plant.

Hindu A person who follows Hinduism.

kirigami A kind of origami where paper can be cut as well as folded.

mantel A structure of wood, marble, or stone above and around a fireplace.

mehndi The practice of painting patterns onto the skin with a dye made from the henna plant.

murti A statue of a deity used in worship.

offerings Things given as gifts to the gods during worship.

procession A crowd of people moving steadily forward along a route.

prosperity Wealth and riches.

rangoli Traditional Indian decorative patterns drawn on the ground with ground rice, flour, and powdered colors, especially at festival times.

samosas Fried, crispy pastries with a spicy meat or vegetable filling.

stepmother A woman who is married to a man who has children from another relationship.

temples Places of worship.

traditions Things that people of a particular place do often or regularly at a certain time of year.

Further Reading

Books

Heiligman, Deborah. *Celebrate Divali: With Sweets, Lights, and Fireworks* (Holidays Around the World). Washington, D.C.: National Geographic Children's Books, 2008.

Murray, Julie. *Divali* (Holidays). Pinehurst, NC: Buddy Books, 2014.

Torpie, Kate. *Divali* (Celebrations in My World). St. Catharines, ON: Crabtree Publishing Company, 2008.

Websites

Due to the changing nature of Internet links, PowerKids Press has developed an online list of websites related to the subject of this book. This site is updated regularly. Please use this link to access the list: **www.powerkidslinks.com/oh/diwali**

Index

A
Ayodhya, 5–6

B
Brahman, 4

D
Deepavali, 6
deities, 7, 18
diya, 6–8

G
Ganges River, 7

I
India, 7, 12

J
Jains, 25

K
Kali, 4

L
Lakshmi, 4, 6, 12–13, 19
Lord Mahavira, 25

M
murtis, 7, 12

N
Nepal, 24, 26

R
Rama, 4–6, 13
rangoli, 19
Ravana, 5

S
Sikhs, 25
Sita, 4–6, 13
Swanti, 24

T
temples, 6–7, 12, 19, 25
Tihar, 24